USBORNE

GEORGIAN HOUSE PICTURE BOOK

Illustrated by Maja Kastelic and Yoko Sugiyama

Written by Abigail Wheatley
Designed by Lucy Wain

Historical consultants:
Treve Rosoman FSA
Emily Parker

Contents

Floor Plan

A country gentleman, his wife and family live in this charming house, along with their servants. The walls of the house have been removed here, so you can see all the rooms inside.

Top Floor

The children of the family - John, Lucy and baby Frances - play in the nursery. Servants sleep across the landing.

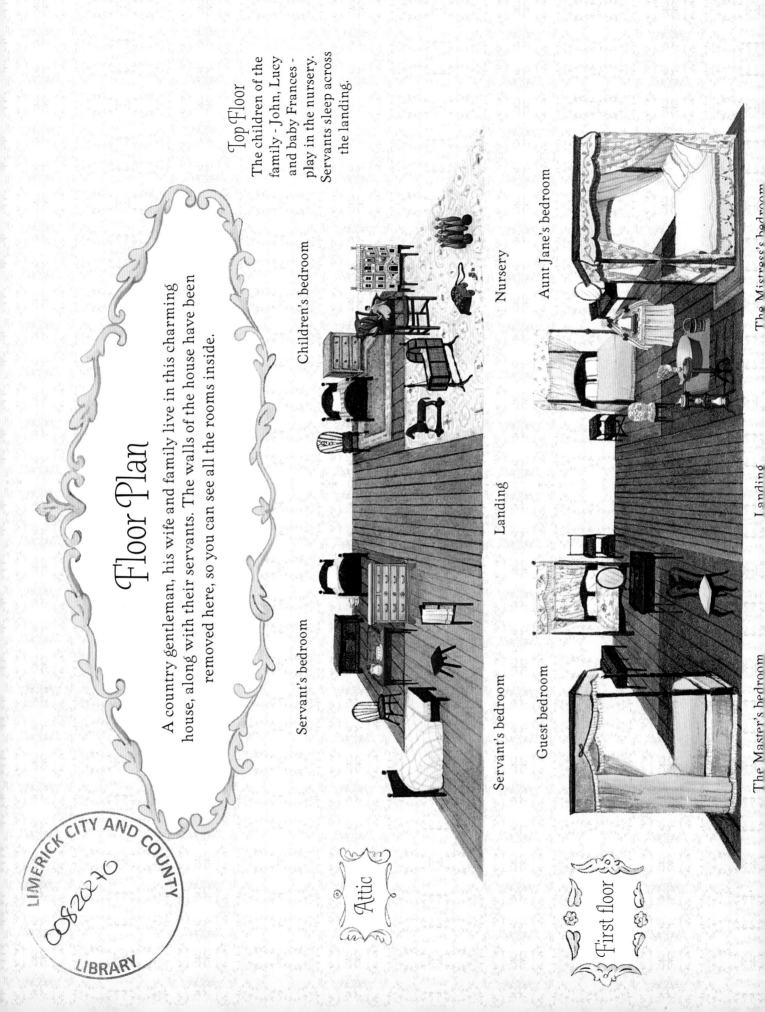

Children's bedroom

Nursery

Servant's bedroom

Attic

Landing

Aunt Jane's bedroom

Servant's bedroom

Guest bedroom

The Master's bedroom

The Mistress's bedroom

Landing

First floor

Ground floor

Living space
The Master spends his days reading in the library, while the Mistress and Aunt Jane play music in the parlour. The drawing room is for evening relaxation.

Library

Drawing room

Parlour

Entrance hall

Dining room

Basement

Below stairs
The kitchen is always full of bustle and steam, keeping the family supplied with food. Supplies are stored in the pantry.

Pantry - food is stored here.

Housekeeper's room

Kitchen

Carriage House

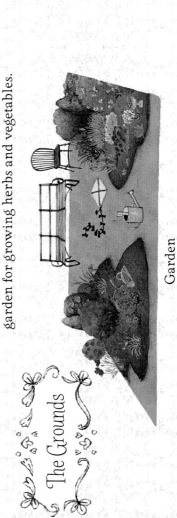

Living space for groom and gardener

Stabling for horses and carriage

The Grounds

As well as a garden for the family to relax in, there is an orchard, and a kitchen garden for growing herbs and vegetables.

Garden

A type of wall clock, called a lantern clock, sits on its wooden bracket.

Family portraits decorate the staircase walls.

Mirrors were very expensive, and only wealthy people could afford them.

The Entrance Hall

The front door opens into the hall of the house. The butler takes visitors' hats and coats, and visitors wait in the hall until the Master or Mistress of the house is ready to receive them in the drawing room.

Candles burn
in the hanging
lantern.

Visitors'
coats, hat
and cane

Longcase
clock

The Master's dogs are
usually not allowed in
the main rooms.

5

The Dining Room

The dining table is set for a celebration dinner, decorated with fruit and flowers from the kitchen garden. Soon the room will be filled with the sound of chatter and laughter.

A vast pink blancmange is waiting for the pudding course.

A sideboard holds silver cutlery.

A set of mahogany chairs surrounds the table.

An expensive hand-woven carpet covers the floor.

Family portraits

A small wooden
clock, called a
bracket clock

Two mahogany and
brass side cabinets have
cupboards containing china
plates and dishes.

A crisp white linen
tablecloth covers
the dining table.

The table is set with
blue and white china
plates and dishes.

The Master and
Mistress of the house
sit at each end of
the table.

A thick linen floorcloth
painted in linseed oil protects
the carpet from any spilt food
and drink.

The Parlour

In Georgian times, the parlour is where the family spend much of their time. They read, write letters, play cards, chat about the day's events and play musical instruments to while away the evenings.

Desk for writing letters

Easel and paintbox

Fan to keep cool

Sometimes the pet birds are allowed to fly around.

Oil lamps

Clavichord

Harp

This small table contains cotton thread and wool for sewing and embroidery.

Portable
writing slope

Folio stand
for large
papers

The Library

The library is probably the quietest room in the house. Here the Master writes letters, studies his books and reads about the latest scientific discoveries. Sometimes Mopsie the cat creeps in to keep him company.

Small bust of a famous writer

This globe shows the Earth, and the other the stars.

Library steps

Mopsie the cat

The Drawing Room

Originally known as a 'withdrawing' room, the drawing room is where visitors are taken, and where the family and their friends withdraw to after lunch or dinner.

A fox hunting scene

A woollen shawl is welcome on a chilly evening.

Porcelain from China was very popular in Georgian times.

Table set for tea and cards

Mirrors with
candles throw
more light into
the room.

Embroidery
frame

Daughter
Lucy's doll

Box
containing
woollen
thread for
embroidery

A coal fire
burns in
the grate.

13

The Kitchen

The kitchen is the busiest, and noisiest, room in the house. The fire rages, the kettle whistles and copper pots and pans clatter and clang. Cook snaps orders as her dishes are whisked away to the dining room.

A huge fireplace dominates the room. It is fed with wood and coal.

A chicken is being roasted on the spit.

Wooden water buckets

Coal scuttle

A copper pan collects juices from the roasting chicken.

Meat pies and stewed fruit are ready to go.

Copper food moulds

Sugar nips cut off chunks of sugar from the sugar loaf.

14

'Bottle jack' for roasting large joints

Pestle and mortar for grinding spices

Elaborate meat pie

This solid block of sugar is known as a 'loaf'.

Copper pan for steaming fish

Four poster bed

Curtains on the bed can be closed for extra warmth.

The Mistress's wig on its stand

Inside the night stand is a chamber pot, which is used as a lavatory.

A portrait of the Mistress's sister hangs beside the dressing table.

Wash stand

Dressing table with perfumes and powders

Her favourite dog, Jewel, waits to greet her.

Fire irons and bellows

The Mistress's Bedroom

During the day, the Mistress wears a wig and elaborate clothes. Every morning her maid draws back the curtains, arranges her clothes for her to choose and powders her wig ready for another day.

The Servant's Bedroom

The servants' bedrooms are at the top of the house. It's colder up here, but they have fires in their rooms and it's always a relief to lie down after a hard day's work.

Servant's family pictures

Bucket for carrying water for washing

Chest with fresh clothes

Simple wooden bed, with a horsehair mattress

A wooden towel rail with cotton towel

High chair

Baby Frances's cradle

Baby house

Wooden wagon with building blocks

Miniature tea set

John's pull-along horse

The Nursery

Across the landing is the nursery, where the children of the family play. They spend much of the day here with their nurse. She makes sure that they are looking their best when they go downstairs to see their parents late in the morning.

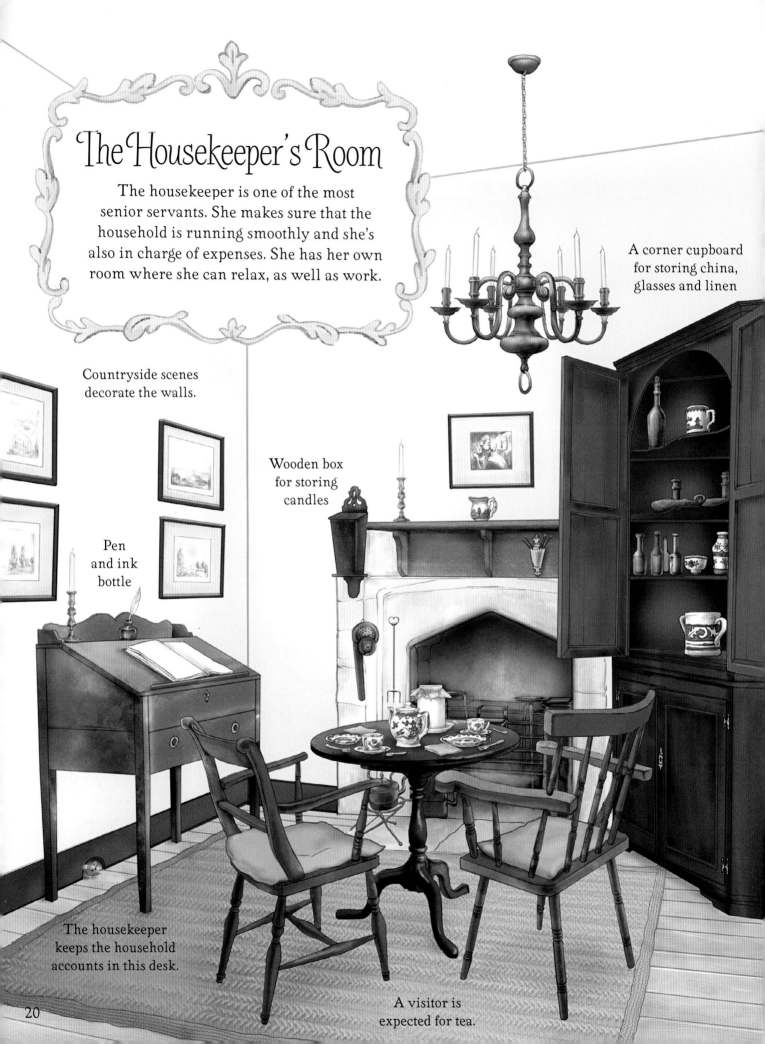

The Housekeeper's Room

The housekeeper is one of the most senior servants. She makes sure that the household is running smoothly and she's also in charge of expenses. She has her own room where she can relax, as well as work.

A corner cupboard for storing china, glasses and linen

Countryside scenes decorate the walls.

Wooden box for storing candles

Pen and ink bottle

The housekeeper keeps the household accounts in this desk.

A visitor is expected for tea.

Jugs and cooking pots are often stored in the pantry.

Jars of preserved vegetables and fruit are used during the winter months.

An impressive collection of copper pans

This wooden chest is used for preparing bread.

Handle pumps water.

Stone sink for washing pots

The floor is covered in thick stone slabs which help to keep the room cool.

The Pantry

The pantry is located near the kitchen, but in a cooler part of the house. It's where food is stored before it is cooked in the kitchen, so the room needs to be as cold as possible in order to keep the food fresh.

The Garden

The house is surrounded by a magnificent garden, with green lawns and colourful flowerbeds. It is the pride of the head gardener and his assistants. The whole family enjoy it during the warm summer.

Stone urn
with flowers

Wrought iron bench

Toy hobby-horse

A stone
roller keeps
the lawn
smooth.

Shears for
clipping

Gate to the
front garden

Mopsie the
cat soaks up
the sun.

Wooden hoop
and stick

A hedgehog looks for
slugs and worms to eat.

Apple and pear trees

Beehives for honey

Neat lines of lettuces
and other salad crops

The Kitchen Garden

Enclosed by high brick walls, the kitchen garden is a very important
part of the house and its grounds. This is where fruit and vegetables
are grown. The walls help keep the area warm throughout the year.

Delicate fruits, such as grapes, are grown in the glasshouse.

Gravel paths lead between the different vegetable beds.

Pumpkins, herbs, leeks and cabbages are all growing here.

The dipping pool in the middle of the garden supplies water for the vegetables and flowerbeds.

The Carriage House

Away from the main house is the carriage house and stableyard, where the family's carriage and horses live. They are looked after by the groom who sleeps in the room above.

The carriage waits to be harnessed to the horses for the next journey into town.

Leather horse harnesses

The groom and the assistant gardener sleep above.

Clean bedlinen on shelves

The horses have plenty of hay to eat.

The horses' droppings are taken away in a wheelbarrow.

27

The Servants

The bigger the house, the greater the number of servants. Both male and female staff are divided into 'upper' and 'under' ranks. At the top is the butler and housekeeper, who keep an eye on all the others.

The housekeeper is in charge of all the other female servants, and makes sure they do their jobs properly. She keeps the keys to many of the cupboards in the house.

The valet helps the Master of the house to dress in the morning. He brushes his clothes and makes sure they are clean and in good order.

The footman has lots of different jobs. He carries coal to the rooms for the fires, cleans and prepares the lamps and helps the butler to serve lunch and dinner.

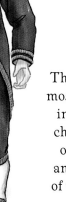

The butler is one of the most important servants in the house. He is in charge of the footmen, orders the wine and announces the arrival of visitors to the house.

The cook is in charge of the kitchen and provides everyone in the house, including the servants, with delicious meals.

The head gardener is in charge of both the main garden, and the kitchen garden where the fruit and vegetables are grown.

In larger households, a kitchen maid helps the cook, preparing meat and vegetables and baking bread.

The housemaid keeps all the rooms clean and tidy. She lights the fires, sweeps the floors and polishes the wooden furniture.

The groom keeps the stables and carriage clean and feeds and exercises the horses.

The coachman drives the carriage. He makes sure the carriage is in good condition and the horses are fed.

The nurse is in charge of caring for the children of the house, feeding and dressing them.

A laundry maid spends her day washing the family's clothes and table linen, and then ironing them.

29

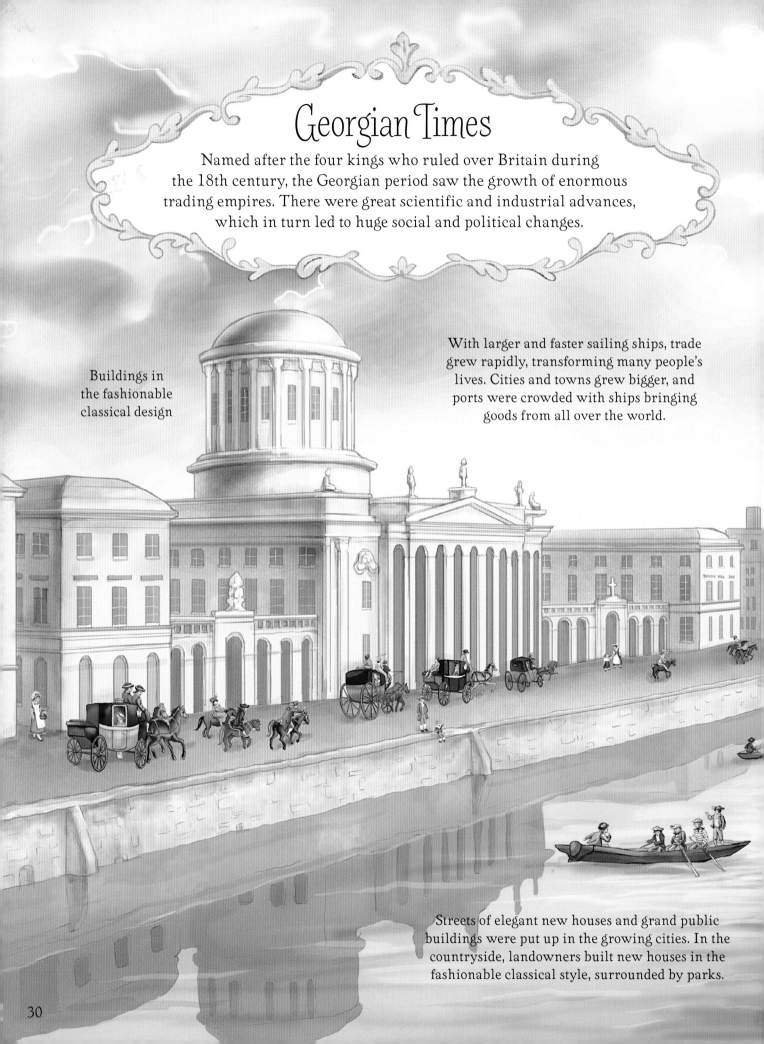

Georgian Times

Named after the four kings who ruled over Britain during the 18th century, the Georgian period saw the growth of enormous trading empires. There were great scientific and industrial advances, which in turn led to huge social and political changes.

Buildings in the fashionable classical design

With larger and faster sailing ships, trade grew rapidly, transforming many people's lives. Cities and towns grew bigger, and ports were crowded with ships bringing goods from all over the world.

Streets of elegant new houses and grand public buildings were put up in the growing cities. In the countryside, landowners built new houses in the fashionable classical style, surrounded by parks.

The Georgian era saw the beginnings of an industrial revolution. Factories with new tools and machines powered by water produced ever greater quantities of goods.

There was a revolution in agriculture. Farmers used new machines and planting methods.

New breeding methods produced much bigger sheep, pigs and cattle.

Scientists made new discoveries about the universe and the world around them. They formed societies where they shared their findings and gave lectures.

New, stronger and smoother roads made travel easier and quicker. Waterways called canals were dug to carry goods from city to city and to ports for export all around the world.

31

Index

Usborne Quicklinks

For links to websites where you can see inside some real Georgian
houses in Britain and find out about everyday life in Georgian times,
go to the Usborne Quicklinks website at
www.usborne.com/quicklinks and type in the title of this book.
Please follow the internet safety guidelines at the Usborne
Quicklinks website.

Additional text: Struan Reid   Additional design: Nelupa Hussain
Digital manipulation: Nick Wakeford   Edited by Jane Chisholm